411

Ripley's Believe It or Not!

Developed and produced by Ripley Publishing Ltd

This edition published and distributed by:
Mason Crest Publishers Inc.
370 Reed Road, Broomall, Pennsylvania 19008
(866) MCP-BOOK (toll free)
www.masoncrest.com

Ripley's Believe it or Not!
Unusual Tales
ISBN 978-1-4222-2028-3 (hardcover)
ISBN 978-1-4222-2062-7 (paperback)

Library of Congress Cataloging-in-Publication data is available

Ripley's Believe it or Not!—Complete 16 Title Series
ISBN 978-1-4222-2014-6

1st printing
10 9 8 7 6 5 4 3 2 1

Library of Congress Cataloging-in-Publication Data is available.
Printed in USA

PUBLISHER'S NOTE
While every effort has been made to verify the accuracy of the entries in this book, the Publisher's cannot be held responsible for any errors contained in the work. They would be glad to receive any information from readers.

WARNING
Some of the stunts and activities in this book are undertaken by experts and should not be attempted by anyone without adequate training and supervision.

Ripley's Believe It or Not!

The Remarkable... Revealed

UNUSUAL TALES

MC
PUBLISHERS

Mason Crest Publishers

UNUSUAL TALES

Strange stories. Get sucked into an astounding

collection of weird legends and mysterious

myths. Find out about the kitten with two heads,

two noses and four eyes, the carthorse that likes

nothing better than a drink at the local pub, and

the girl who has been pulling glass from her

head every day for three years.

Davison Design and Development has provided its
employees with an "Inventionland" workspace...

FISHY TALES

Florida-based artist Juan Cabana creates his own fantastic mermaids and sea monsters from fish and animal remains.

He wraps fish and animal skins around steel, plastic, and fiberglass frames, often adding alligator claws for the hands and monkey skulls for the heads. One of his biggest creations—a mermaid nearly 7 ft (2.1 m) long—had the body of a 100-lb (45-kg) grouper.

His interest began several years ago when he acquired an old Japanese-made Fiji mermaid on the Internet auction site eBay. "Just holding the mermaid, I felt the energy and power. I was hooked and decided to continue the tradition of making these creatures." At first he tried to copy the originals, but then developed his own style.

The shape and size of each creature depends on the materials he has available. "I don't kill any fish or animals. I get my fish skins from a local market, where they would otherwise be thrown away. At first I was revolted by handling fish skins but gradually I got used to them. I also had to learn taxidermy."

Each mermaid can take weeks to build. "Rather than looking fresh and alive, my creations are supposed to look old, mummified, and withered, as if they had been found washed up on a beach. I invent a story for each mermaid, saying that I found it on a particular beach rather than just saying I made it."

One of Cabana's mermaids is seen here looking as if it had washed up on a beach.

RIPLEY'S RESEARCH

Tales of mermaids date back centuries. However, the most famous mermaid of all was the Fiji mermaid, brought to New York in 1842 by a mysterious Englishman, Dr. J. Griffin, who claimed it had been caught by Japanese fishermen. In truth, Griffin was an associate of the renowned showman, P.T. Barnum, and the mermaid was nothing more than a monkey's head and body sewn onto a fish's tail. Even so, huge crowds paid 25 cents a head to see Barnum's mysterious mermaid.

LIGHTER LIT!
The government building in Astana, Kazakhstan, known by locals as "The Cigarette Lighter" because of its shape, caught fire on May 30, 2006.

HEBREW COIN
After shopping at her local supermarket in Sumter, South Carolina, Lynn Moore noticed something odd in her change. She knew it wasn't a penny, but she was very surprised to hear the news from a coin expert that the coin was probably from ancient Hebrew society, and was minted around 135AD.

HAMSTER HOME
In May 2006, as revenge for a practical joke, Luke Trerice's friends turned his apartment in Olympia, Washington, into a giant hamster cage! The cage featured an exercise wheel that was 6 ft (1.8 m) in diameter, shredded newspaper on the floor, and a huge water bottle. In 2004, Trerice had wrapped the entire contents of a friend's apartment in tin foil!

MISSED MONOLITH
A 44-year-old Australian man was arrested for drunk-driving in March 2006 after asking police the way to Uluru—when he was parked just 330 ft (100 m) from the world's largest monolith with his headlights pointing straight at it. The Uluru landmark, also known as Ayers Rock, rises 1,115 ft (340 m) above the Australian desert and is 6 mi (9.6 km) around.

RICKSHAW ROBOT

Over the last 26 years Wu Yulu, a Chinese farmer from Beijing, has built 25 robots out of scrap metal, screws, nails, and wire from rubbish dumps. Some models light cigarettes, others serve tea, and this particular one, which took him a year to build, pulls rickshaws. "Humanoid robot rickshaw" stands 6 ft (1.8 m) high and has Ping-Pong eyes and a sponge mouth. There is a steering wheel on the rickshaw with a control button that controls the robot's movement. Powered by electricity, it is capable of moving forwards and backwards for 6 hours covering 5 mi (8 km), taking 30 to 40 steps a minute.

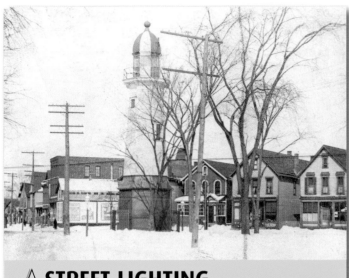

⚠ STREET LIGHTING

A lighthouse once stood in the middle of a residential street in Niagara Falls, New York. It was torn down during the winter of 1933–34.

EMERGENCY LANDING

In September 2006, a light airplane made an emergency landing on a busy street in the heart of Montreal, Canada. The Cessna's engine had cut out during an aerial tour of the city, forcing the pilot to touch down safely on Parc Avenue, a main north–south thoroughfare, in front of dozens of baffled onlookers. The only damage was to a street sign clipped by one of the plane's wings.

PIG PONG

The entire village of Elsa in southern Germany was flooded by pig manure when a storage tank with a capacity of 63,400 gal (240,000 l) burst in February 2006.

SUSPICIOUS MINDS

Texas farmers near the Mexican border have erected ladders to allow illegal immigrants to climb over their fences. The move was designed to stop them cutting holes in the fences, which allowed the farmers' cattle to escape. However, most of the illegal immigrants have apparently been ignoring the ladders because they think it's a trick!

OCTOPUS WRESTLING

Eric Morris of Port Orchard, Washington, regularly wrestles giant Pacific octopuses in Puget Sound and at the World Octopus Wrestling Championships each year in Tacoma, Washington.

BOG JOG

A jogger who took a wrong turn during a 2006 lunchtime run in Florida ended up stuck in a swamp for four days. Training for the Baltimore Marathon, 62-year-old Eddie Meadows left his desk at the University of Central Florida's research park every lunchtime to jog around the campus. But on this occasion he got lost, fell into a bog, and survived only by sipping water from the swamp.

ELDERLY ROBBER

A 79-year-old woman was arrested in Chicago, Illinois, in 2006 after she tried to hold up a bank at gunpoint. Brandishing a toy gun and demanding $30,000 cash, she told the cashier she wasn't able to speak very loudly because she had just come from the dentist.

TREE-MENDOUS OFFICE △

Davison Design and Development, a product design company based in Pittsburgh, Pennsylvania, has provided its employees with a tree house, the insides of a robot, and a pirate ship as creative spaces within which to work, known as "Inventionland." The tree house is actually an area of trees, the first of which is about 20 ft (6 m) in diameter with a tunnel carved into it through which workers pass on their way across a bridge of water to get to the elevated "house" standing 15 ft (4.5 m) high. A porch in the tree house overlooks a lake and a waterfall.

CELEBRITY DELUSION

A Canadian drunk driver escaped conviction in 2006 because he believed Shania Twain was helping him to drive. The 33-year-old man was arrested for speeding in downtown Ottawa, but a judge ruled him not criminally responsible because he suffered from delusions that female celebrities were communicating with him telepathically.

GOLD DIGGER

When his gold detector picked up a signal near the front patio of his home in Montclair, California, in 2006, 63-year-old Henry Mora started digging. He intended excavating only a few feet but as the detector kept bleeping, Henry kept digging. Eventually, worried authorities were forced to stop him after he created a hole 60 ft (18 m) deep! He admitted he had got "carried away."

CAT KILLER

A woman from Miami Gardens, Florida, had been searching for her one-year-old Siamese cat for two days in 2005 when her son discovered a bulging python slithering in the family's backyard. An X ray on the snake showed that it had indeed eaten a cat.

MINNOW MYSTERY

Biologists at the University of Manchester found this duck egg in a small pond in the French Alps. They noticed something moving inside and when they cracked open the shell discovered three live minnows inside! They were baffled as to how the minnows got inside. There appeared to be no crack in the egg.

FLUTE MELTED

A Swedish orchestra playing instruments carved from ice had to abandon a 2006 concert after the flutist's warm breath caused her flute to melt! Tim Linharts had made functioning flutes, violins, and a double bass out of ice for the performance in a large igloo in the town of Pitea.

EXCUSED DUTY

A 103-year-old Canadian woman was excused from serving her jury duty in 2006 because it would have interfered with her afternoon nap. Phyllis Perkins from Saskatoon, Saskatchewan, asked to be excluded on the grounds that she needed her regular daytime doze.

PARKING FINE

A Florida motorist finally paid his parking fine—60 years after getting it. William Fogarty, now 87, received the ticket in Norfolk, Virginia, in May 1946. He bought a $1 money order to pay the fine but forgot to send it off. When he was clearing out an old box in 2006, he found the money order and mailed it.

◁ FAKE CRASH

A California man staged a fake plane crash in his own garden— as a Halloween stunt! Complete with false human legs sticking out the bottom, the scene was so realistic it even fooled the police. Inspired by the TV series *Lost*, Steve Chambers picked up the parts of a G3 Gulfstream jet from the factory in Van Nuys where he works as an aviation mechanic. He sealed off the site with yellow caution tape and added a sign reading: "Do not enter: Under investigation."

WINTER BLUES

In 2006, Dr. Alex Bobak converted the waiting room in his London office into a beach to help patients beat the winter blues.

He transformed the space into a Caribbean-style paradise where waiting room chairs were swapped for sun loungers, palm trees, sand, and sun. Several light-therapy lights were brought in to replicate the sun's rays.

HOSPITAL WEDDING

Rev. Don Hoover of Lincoln, Illinois, conducted the marriage of Janel Hoover and Ed Tibbits at the hospital emergency room where he'd been taken after developing severe leg cramps.

ANGER BAR

A new bar that has opened in the Chinese city of Nanjing allows stressed-out customers to unleash pent-up anger by attacking staff, smashing glasses, and generally causing mayhem! The Rising Sun Anger Release Bar employs 20 strong young men as "models" for customers to punch and scream at.

BAR HORSE ▷

Peggy, the carthorse, regularly joins her owner Peter Dolan for a pint of beer and pickled onion potato chips at the Alexandra Hotel in Jarrow, England. She used to be tied up with a long rope outside the pub, but one day followed her owner into the bar and stayed for a drink.

SPLASHED CASH

When Vanisha Mittal married Amit Bhatia in Paris, France, her father, billionaire industrialist Lakshmi Mittal, rented the Tuileries Garden at Versailles and Louis XIV's chateau for a wedding celebration that cost $60 million.

PANCAKE FOLLY

A man from Bensalem, Pennsylvania, who robbed a bank in 2006 and escaped with around $4,000, was caught when he stopped for pancakes. Police said the man might have got away with the raid on a Bank of America branch had he not stopped for a snack at the nearby Sunrise Diner.

CHEESY ATTRACTION

U.S. Navy Petty Officer Mike Evans opened a bag of Cheetos and discovered a giant cheese snack the size of a lemon. He then donated the cheesy lump to the town of Algona, Iowa, to be used as a tourist attraction.

PET SOUP

A 2006 survey showed that one in three dog owners in South Korea enjoys boshintang soup, which is made from dog meat. It is said to aid stamina and virility.

HEFTY HERO

When a teenage cyclist was trapped under a car in Tucson, Arizona, in July 2006, he was saved by a strong bystander who lifted the car right off the ground. At 6 ft 4 in (1.93 m) tall and weighing 300 lb (136 kg), Tom Boyle raised the Chevrolet Camaro single-handedly, allowing the driver to haul the injured cyclist clear.

KITCHEN TRAP

A Czech man avoided jail for four years by hiding under the floorboards in his mother's kitchen. Police finally caught up with him on a surprise visit to the house when they spotted him trying to slide through a trap door into a vacant cellar.

ALCOHOLIC LAKE

Following a malfunction at a nearby distillery in June 2006, Bracholinksie Lake in Wielkopolska, Poland, was reported to have concentrations of vodka as high as 30 per cent.

◁ CAT WITH 12 CLAWS

This five-month-old cat called Bigfoot from Brooklet, Georgia, has six claws on each of its front feet. It was born of normal parents.

FLOCK OF SEAGULLS

A flock of several hundred gull-like shearwaters crashed into a fishing boat for half an hour off the coast of Alaska in the early hours of August 30, 2006. More than 1,600 bird carcasses were found washed up on the nearby shores of the town of Unalaska over the next two days. Flocks of shearwaters can number a million birds and some species are attracted to lights on boats.

WEDDING FRAUD

A Japanese man and woman were sent to prison in 2006 for falsely claiming that he was of royal descent and for staging a lavish wedding to collect gift money from unsuspecting guests. They had apparently swindled over $25,000 in gift money from 61 guests at their 2003 wedding reception.

BABY NAMES

A Belgian couple expecting their 15th baby put an ad in an Antwerp newspaper because they had run out of ideas for names. Brigitte Dillen and Ivo Driessens had given all of their children names ending in a "y" but after Wendy, Cindy, Jimmy, Brendy, Sonny, Sandy, Purdy, Chardy, Yorry, Yony, Britney, Yenty, Ruby, and Xanty, they were unable to come up with any new suggestions.

TRASH FIND

Dropping off his household trash at a dump site, Michael Hoskins of Danville, Virginia, spotted a pile of old books waiting to be thrown away. Among them he discovered a 188-year-old King James Bible, one of less than half a dozen copies belived to be in existence.

CHARITY RECEPTION

A scorned bride canceled her September 2006 wedding and turned the reception into a charity event. After learning that her fiancé had been cheating on her, Kyle Paxman decided to salvage something positive from the disappointment by inviting 125 women and making the reception at Lake Champlain, Vermont, a charity benefit.

GOLF SHAME

A caddy at a golf course in Long Island, New York, was awarded $34,000 in a sexual harassment lawsuit in 2006 after he was ridiculed by his boss for losing two golf matches to a woman.

ROOSTER SILENCED

In 2006, a Scottish council sought an Anti-Social Behaviour Order on a rooster that crowed too early and too loudly. Since Charlie's crowing apparently exceeded the 30-decibel limit set by the World Health Organization, Borders Council demanded that his owner, Kenneth Williamson, keep the bird silent between 11 p.m. and 7 a.m.

PIECE OF MIND

Sambhu Roy of India survived an electrical accident with severe burns to his skull. His scalp was completely burned and several months later, reportedly, a piece of his skull fell off. The inner covering of the skull was unaffected and new bone had grown and pushed the dead skull out. Sambhu has kept the old piece of skull as a personal trophy.

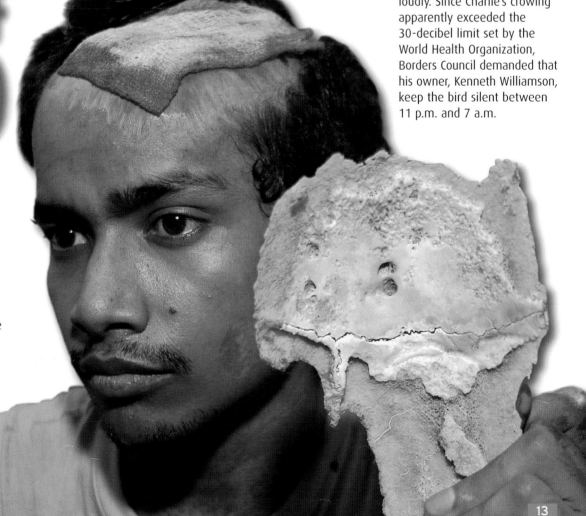

MISSING KEY

A locksmith from North Platte, Nebraska, made a key to this man's truck from an X ray that the local hospital made when the man swallowed the key. The new key worked on the first try!

UNUSUAL DIET ▷

R. F. Durga swallowed all of these metal objects, which included a fish hook, three pocket knives, five rifle shells, 17 horseshoe nails, a collection of coins and keys, and various pieces of broken glass. He underwent surgery in 1908 to remove the items from his stomach.

BITING THE BULLET

A 73-year-old Inuit woman was hospitalized in Nome, Alaska, after an abdominal X ray revealed that her appendix was filled with buckshot. Doctors said Inuits hunt so many ducks and geese for food that some of the buckshot remains in the cooked meat and is then eaten and digested.

DRANK COINS

Gigi Florin of Romania was hospitalized after swallowing 120 coins washed down with wine—the result of a bet he made with a friend. He thought the wine would help digest the coins, but then collapsed.

KNIFE SWALLOWER

Mao Kyan from Chendu in China had a 3-in (7.6-cm) knife stuck in his throat for eight months. He had swallowed the knife during a police raid on his flat to avoid being charged with possessing a weapon.

ALIEN VISITOR

When the International Bird Rescue Research Center in Cordelia, California, treated an injured duck in May 2006, an X ray revealed what looked like the face of ET in the bird's stomach. The Center planned to auction the "unbelievable" X ray to raise funds.

CLOSE SHAVE

A 61-year-old Mesa, Arizona, man was shot in the face while sleeping. He didn't realize what had happened until three days later when the bullet showed up in an X ray.

FALL GUY

A retired Polish schoolteacher went to the hospital hoping to be given painkillers to relieve his headache, but instead doctors pulled a 5-in (13-cm) knife blade out of his head. The knife had pierced Leonard Woronowicz's skull when he had fallen over a stool in his kitchen. All he noticed was a small gash on his head, so he put a bandage on it. He wasn't even suspicious when he couldn't find the kitchen knife the following day.

LIFE SAVER

A police officer in Serbia, saved an old lady's life after she accidentally swallowed a set of false teeth while eating a sandwich. The passing policeman thought the woman had choked on the sandwich, but when he squeezed her diaphragm the pair of dentures flew out of her mouth.

MISLAID SCISSORS

Australian Pat Skinner got a shock when she saw this X ray of her pelvis in 2004. It showed a pair of surgical scissors that had been left inside her body during an operation she'd had 18 months previously.

SNAKE X RAY ▷

In July 2006, a yellow rat snake was found in a chicken coop in Homosassa, Florida, suffering from severe indigestion after having swallowed a golf ball. The snake was taken to Midway Animal Hospital in the town, where it underwent life-saving surgery to remove the offending object—it would not have been able to digest or pass the solid ball, and would have died without the operation.

▽ UNFINISHED OP

Donald Church from Lynnwood, Washington, survived a surgical mishap when a surgical retractor 13 in (33 cm) long and 2 in (5 cm) wide was accidentally left in his body.

△ SEVERE HEADACHE

Isidro Mejia from California had six nails removed from his head and neck after nails from a nail gun were shot into his head in 2004. Five of the six nails were removed in surgery immediately and the sixth was removed from his face when the swelling went down.

TIME CAPSULE

A message in a bottle that had remained hidden in a wall at Quonset Naval Air Station, Rhode Island, for 65 years was finally unearthed in 2006. It had been written in 1941 by two carpenters who were part of a civilian army hired to build military bases in the area. The message asked, "Will this bottle see the sun?" With its discovery came the answer.

BURNING HEART

To demonstrate his love for his girlfriend, Hannes Pisek made a huge heart out of 220 burning candles on the floor of his apartment in Hoenigsberg, Austria. Sadly, while he was collecting her from work, his burning heart set fire to the apartment. He not only lost his home but also his girl who promptly went back to live with her parents.

TONGUE VISION

Although he has been blind since birth, Mike Ciarciello can "see" through his tongue. In 2006, researchers at Canada's University of Montreal mounted a small camera on his forehead, which sent electrical impulses about what it saw to a small grid placed on his tongue. As a result, he was able to walk through a tricky obstacle course without a cane. "It's a concept in which you replace a sense that was lost by another one that is there," explained supervising neuropsychologist Maurice Ptito. "They sense the world through their tongue, and that gives them the feeling of seeing. You don't see with your eyes. You see with your brain."

PARKING ROW

A street parking attendant in Rio de Janeiro, Brazil, was charged in 2006 with sawing a woman in two over a parking space dispute. Police said the man murdered the 51-year-old businesswoman following an argument after she had parked her car in a prohibited spot.

△ IT'S FISH AGAIN!

In 1941, Adolph Flashner was known as "King of the Sea," because he ate fish at every single mealtime, including breakfast. He also claimed never to have eaten meat in his life.

POOR PLANNING

Two thieves from Cincinnati, Ohio, might have got away with stealing a flat-screen TV measuring 55 in (1.4 m) wide from a store in Middletown, Ohio—if only they had brought a bigger getaway car. Instead they made their escape in a tiny Mercury Sable with the TV hanging out of the open rear door, and were quickly spotted by police.

◁ MILK FOR THE GODS

August 2006 saw Hindu temples across northern India thronged with devotees all coming to see statues of the gods Shiva, Ganesh, and Durga purportedly drinking spoonfuls of milk that were offered to them. At the Shiva temple in Lucknow, priest Sudhir Mishra said that 21 pt (10 l) of milk had been offered to a statue of Shiva and that all of it had been drunk by the god. Indian government scientists said that the milk had disappeared because it had effectively been absorbed by the statue, but this did not stop the rush of pilgrims to the temples.

IN DEPTH
STOMACH FOR A FIGHT

Sonya Thomas is America's competitive eating champion, calling herself the Black Widow. She weighs just 99 lbs (45 kg), but has managed to put away 46 mince pies in ten minutes and 52 hard-boiled eggs in just five!

How did you start competitive eating?

"I eat more than normal people, so I thought it might be something I'd be good at. I won a qualifier for the annual July 4 contest three years ago at Nathan's Famous Hog Dogs on Coney Island, New York. In the final I ate 25 hotdogs with buns in 12 minutes—a new women's record."

Were you a big eater as a child?

"I was born and grew up in South Korea, and only emigrated to America when I was 26. I didn't eat a lot as a child because we were so poor."

Do you feel ill after a contest?

"No—an average contest consumption will only be about 9 lbs of food in 10 or 12 minutes—that's not enough to fill me up!"

Do you have any special training or techniques?

"I do daily aerobic exercise and eat one big, but healthy, meal a day. I drink a lot of water or diet cola with it—maybe 20 glasses—to expand my capacity. And before a big contest, I find out what food it will be and practice eating it fast."

Why do you call yourself the "Black Widow?"

"Eating contests are traditionally all male, and the Black Widow is a female spider that kills and eats her mate! When I started to rank higher and higher in the contests, the men said: 'How can a little woman do that?' I kept beating them and eventually they respected me."

You are only 5 ft 5 in with a tiny frame—have you got an unusual digestive system?

"Most top eaters are not heavy—skinny people have less fat to restrict the stomach. You need a large throat, or esophagus, to get the food down, a strong jaw for chewy foods, and a big stomach capacity. Mine holds 18–20lbs of food."

Is it dangerous—and how do you avoid putting on weight?

"I don't gain weight because I only eat like that once in a while. During contests, there is a danger of choking, but every sport has its injuries. There are always medical people standing by."

What are your favorite contest foods?

"Oysters—46 dozen in 10 minutes. Seafood is the easiest. 11 lbs of cheesecake in nine minutes was one I'm proud of, as well as 46 crab cakes in 10 minutes and 162 buffalo wings in 12 minutes."

Is there anything you won't eat?

"I didn't eat any meat until I was 21. I still don't like it much—especially pork. And I don't like anything too unusual, like frogs' legs! But I don't think about how it tastes—I just think about winning."

How long will you carry on—and what would you like to eat next?

"I hold 27 records, but I will carry on as long as my body can do it. I manage a fast food restaurant—perfect for me! But I want to increase my speed. I want to try sushi, and after that noodles—I think they would go down quickly!"

▽ LOST RING

Mrs. Caroline Scufaca of Canon City, Colorado, was understandably upset on losing her wedding ring in 1923. She had to wait 15 long years before the ring turned up in her garden—on a carrot!

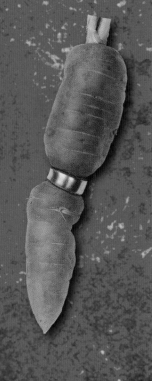

△ TREE TRANSPLANT

This 120-year-old oak tree was one of several large old oaks that were dug up and moved just 500 yd (457 m) from their original home in Spring 2006. A chain store wanted to build on the land in Auburndale, Florida, and had to pay more than $100,000 to have the trees moved under new laws protecting established trees. This tree was the largest to be moved and weighed a colossal 353 tons. It took six weeks to dig out, transport, and move to its new home.

HEARING VOICES

A Japanese man was arrested in 2006 after making 37,760 silent calls to directory enquiries because he enjoyed listening to the "kind" voices of female telephone operators. He made up to 905 calls a day.

INSURANCE CLAIM

English insurance company Norwich Union reached a settlement in 2006 with one of its employees, Linda Riley, over her workplace injuries. Ironically, she had tripped over a pile of claim forms in the office.

WEIRD THEFT

In May 2006, thieves in Germany stole an entire roller coaster! The Big Dipper, weighing 20 tons and worth $25,000, disappeared from a truck that had stopped at a parking lot on its way to a funfair near Bischofsheim.

TREE DWELLER

An Indian man has spent 50 years in a tree after a fight with his wife. Gayadhar Parida, now 84, took to staying in a mango tree after the quarrel and, although he moved trees when his original tree house was destroyed in a storm, he has steadfastly refused to return to the family home in Kuligaon, Orissa. He accepts food offered to him by family members but comes down only to drink water from a pool.

COURT RULING

Believing that posing for photos is sinful, Canada's small Hutterite religious community won a court ruling in May 2006 to acquire driver's licences without identity pictures.

DUNG SOUVENIR ▷

A zoo in Chiang Mai, Thailand, has found a novel way to earn a little extra money, by turning giant panda dung into paper to make souvenirs. Pandas at the Chiang Mai Zoo are fed chopped bamboo and excrete around 50 lbs (23 kg) of waste a day, which is primarily composed of bamboo pulp that the pandas cannot digest. This pulp is then turned into paper using traditional papermaking methods.

LITTER SPILL

A major road in California had to be temporarily closed in 2006 after a truck carrying ten tons of cat litter overturned and spilled its load. It took four hours to clean up the mess, spread across two lanes of the Golden State Freeway in Sun Valley.

$10,000 TIP

For Hutchinson, Kansas, restaurant waitress Cindy Kienow, three years of attentive service to a customer paid off in spectacular fashion in 2006 when he left her a $10,000 tip on a $26 dinner—that's over 38,000 per cent of the cost of the meal! Miss Kienow said the regular was always a generous tipper. "He said, 'This will buy you something kind of nice, huh?' And I said, 'Yeah, it will.' I didn't know what to say."

FORGERY FAILED

A man in Thunder Bay, Ontario, Canada, was arrested for forging a prescription in 2004 after the pharmacy staff decided it was too legible and called the police.

GIRL TALK

CNN viewers were able to listen to news presenter Kyra Phillips's private cell phone conversation about her family in 2006 after she forgot to switch off the microphone she was wearing when she went to the washroom. Her thoughts on her "passionate" husband and "control freak" sister-in-law were broadcast live, loud and clear, and drowned out a speech by President George W. Bush.

SKUNK DETERRENT

In order to keep trespassers out of condemned buildings, Richland County deputies in South Carolina use simulated skunk odor as a deterrent.

PILOT STRANDED

Half an hour from the end of a flight from Ottawa to Winnipeg in 2006, the plane's pilot took a bathroom break, only to find himself locked out of the cockpit on his return. After he had banged on the cockpit door for 10 minutes, the crew were forced to remove the faulty door from its hinges in order to let him back in.

IN A FLAP

The escape of a chicken from a farm in Nuberg, South Carolina, in 2006 caused widespread damage to an adjoining property. Six large cows on the neighboring farm were spooked by the flapping chicken and stampeded out of their barn, half demolishing the building and knocking down several sections of fence.

BIRTHDAY ESCAPE

In Kolasin, Montenegro, a prisoner broke out of jail in 2006 by overpowering guards and scaling a wall 10 ft (3 m) high... just to wish his girlfriend a happy birthday. After going straight to her house and passing on the greetings, he turned himself in to police. He claimed he had been forced to escape because he hadn't been allowed to use the prison phone.

PERKY PENSIONER

A 75-year-old woman chased after a middle-aged man who stole her purse and when she caught up with him, she gave him $3! Betty Horton of South Salt Lake, Utah, said the man had apologized to her, saying he was broke. So after giving him a sound telling off, she handed him some spare change.

WOW, ALICE!

This kitten with two faces was born in Inverness, Florida, in July 2006. She was inspected by veterinarian Dr. Wade Phillips who reported that she had two mouths, both of which were fully functional, two noses, and four eyes. Her owner, Brandy Conley, gave her two names: "Wow," for everyone's first reaction on seeing her, and "Alice," after rock star Alice Cooper. Sadly, Wow Alice did not survive.

LETTER MANIA

AT THE HEIGHT OF ROBERT RIPLEY'S POPULARITY, HE RECEIVED THOUSANDS OF LETTERS FROM AROUND THE WORLD EVERY WEEK TELLING HIM OF UNBELIEVABLE FACTS THAT THE WRITERS HOPED MIGHT BE INCLUDED IN HIS FAMOUS CARTOON STRIP. OVER A PERIOD FROM 1929-31, MANY OF THESE ARRIVED ADDRESSED IN A HIGHLY UNUSUAL FASHION.

In April 1930 the U.S. Postmaster General said that the Post Office would cease to deliver the coded letters to Ripley because postal clerks had had to devote too much time to deciphering the codes!

LETTERS WERE WRITTEN IN ALL LANGUAGES AND DIALECTS. THEY INCLUDED A LETTER ADDRESSED IN RUNIC CODE—THE LANGUAGE OF THE ANCIENT VIKINGS—AND ONE ADDRESSED TO SIMPLY "BELIEVE IT OR NOT!" WRITTEN IN THE OLD CONFEDERATE CIVIL WAR CODE. OTHERS WERE WRITTEN IN SHORTHAND, NUMERIC CODES, SIGN LANGUAGE, INDIAN SIGNS, AND SOME HAD A RIP ON THE FRONT OF THE ENVELOPE TO INDICATE "RIP"-LEY. SOME BORE ONLY QUESTION MARKS, AND MANY HAD RIPPLING LINES DRAWN ACROSS THEM—INDICATING A "RIPPLY" RIVER.

NEWSPAPER ADDICT

Feng Yi from the southern Chinese city of Hefei has collected more than 800,000 copies of 6,000 different types of newspaper from around the world. He plans to open a museum in his hometown to house his collection.

WIFE SOLD

Unable to settle a $3,500 debt, a Romanian man handed over his wife as repayment instead. Emil Iancu signed a document stating that his wife Daniela would live with elderly creditor Jozef Justien Lostrie. Far from being insulted, Mrs. Iancu was delighted by the new arrangement, as she said she no longer had to tidy up after her lazy husband.

GRAVE CONCERN

In 2006, Yahaya Wahab received a phone bill for $218 trillion from Telekom Malaysia for recent calls that had been made—on the line of his dead father! After initially giving him ten days to pay up or face prosecution, the company agreed to look into the matter.

NUTTY PROFESSOR

In January 2006, a harassed professor of history at a Canadian University offered automatic B-minus grades to any students in his overcrowded class if they would simply go away. Twenty of the 95 accepted.

LUCKY SHOT

A 54-year-old man was shot in the abdomen during a robbery in Bakersfield, California, in February 2006, but during surgery doctors found a tumor that otherwise would not have been identified until much later.

LUCKY BEGGAR

His marriage proposal rejected, an angry lover tossed the engagement ring in a beggar's bowl. The recipient, Tim Pockett, who plays the penny whistle for loose change in Shropshire, England, could not believe his luck when the diamond solitaire white gold ring landed in his collection pot. The spurned suitor had told him: "That will keep you going for a couple of days."

◁ DEAD FAMOUS

In 1960, at the age of 14, Charles Hasley from Bowling Green, Kentucky, started collecting obituaries of famous people, and newspaper reports of their deaths, and has been collecting ever since. All of his clippings come from regional rather than national newspapers, and every one is an original.

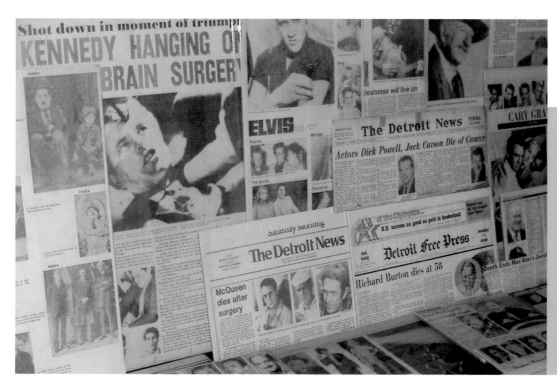

MOM ON STRIKE

Fed up with her unruly, untidy children, a single mother from London, Ontario, Canada, announced in September 2006 that she was going on strike. Mother-of-three Roxanne Toussaint erected a tent and a sign on her front lawn that read "Mom On Strike" and refused to do any further housework until the kids signed a written pledge promising to help out more.

GUARD BAIT

After robbing a Jersey City, New Jersey, bank of more than $4,000 in May 2006, a thief slowed down a pursuing security guard by throwing $20 bills to the ground. As the guard stopped to pick up $1,500 in dropped notes, the robber was able to make his escape.

MANY TONGUES

Although it has a population of only 5.5 million, Papua New Guinea has over 700 spoken languages, most of which are entirely unrelated.

DRACOREX HOGWARTSIA

When the children's museum of Indianapolis, Indiana, had the chance to name a newly discovered species of dinosaur, they referenced Hogwarts, the fictional wizard's school attended by Harry Potter.

DUTCH DILEMMA

Police officers from Bristol, England, were forced to learn Dutch in 2006 because three dogs they recruited from Holland did not respond to commands in English.

△ FAT FISH

In September 2006, Mr. Zhang caught more than he expected while fishing with friends in Shijiazhuang, Hebei province, China. Dangling from the end of his fishing line was a golden fish which, although only 8 in (20 cm) long, had a huge waistline measuring more than 11¾ in (30 cm). It weighed around 1 lb 12 oz (800 g). Nobody knows the reason for its massive stomach.

HARD KICK

During the 2006 World Cup in Germany, two Austrian men were arrested for placing concrete-filled soccer balls around Berlin with signs that encouraged people to kick them.

TITANIC WEDDING

David Leibowitz and Kimberly Miller of New York City were married in a submersible that was resting on the bow of the sunken *Titanic*.

CIGARETTE BREAK

A hospital patient in Berlin, Germany, was stuck in a broken elevator for more than three days in 2006 after sneaking out of bed for a cigarette. Severely dehydrated, 68-year-old Karlheinz Schmidt was finally found after technicians were called to repair the elevator—80 hours after he first got into it.

IN THE PINK ▷

Brumas, a healthy nine-year-old white cat from Devon, England, has inexplicably turned pink. Brumas went for a stroll one day in 2005 and came home with bright pink fur. He was checked out by a veterinarian, who told his owners that the cat was healthy and that the cause of the color change was not toxic. He also told them that it had not been caused by paint, leaving them mystified as to what had really happened.

Can You See It?

SPECIAL DELIVERY

A chicken named Elvis laid an egg signed by The King in Wiltshire, England, in 2005. The egg marked with a perfect letter "K" left farmer John Warwick wondering "maybe Elvis was reborn as a chicken, you never know."

TOAST KING

Maria Morrow was making toast while listening to the Elvis song "Hunk of Burning Love," when she was stunned to see that the toast had an image of The King imprinted on it. The toast was later sold at an art fair for $200.

JESUS TILE

This image of Jesus was spotted on the bathroom wall of a house in Essex, England, in 2005. It appeared on one of a panel of randomly patterned tiles in the home of retired city worker, Philomena Risat.

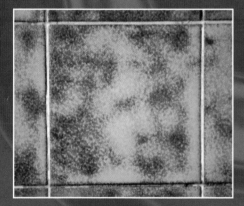

SPIDER-FACE

This spider with markings on its back resembling a human face was found in the city of Wujiaqu in northwestern China in April 2006.

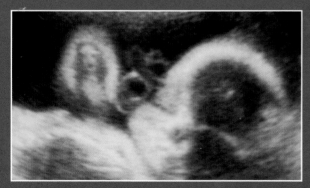

HOLY ULTRASOUND

Studying the latest ultrasound picture of her unborn son, 20-year-old Laura Turner of Warwickshire, England, was amazed to see that it appeared to show an image of Jesus in a shroud.

LITTLE RED ROOSTER

This naturally formed image of a rooster was found in a block of wood about to be used by a wooden stool maker in Shandong province, China, in 2005, which was coincidentally the Chinese Year of the Rooster.

COLLECTIONS

HOUND HAIRPIECES

Ruth Regina of Miami, Florida, runs a boutique that sells wigs for dogs whose owners want them to look sexy! Among her most popular lines are the "Yappy Hour" (a fluff of curls) and the "Peek a Bow Wow," which falls down over part of the dog's face, apparently giving a stylish look reminiscent of 1940s movie star Veronica Lake.

SIMPLE EXPLANATION

When water suddenly began spouting from the base of a statue of the late Pope John Paul II in his hometown of Wadowice, Poland, in 2006, people flocked from all over the country to drink from the "miracle fountain." But the suggestion of divine intervention was shattered when city council officials revealed that it was they who had installed a pipe beneath the statue to make it look prettier.

HEAVY SLEEPERS

A pair of Serbian gas station attendants on night shift slept while thieves broke into their office in 2006 and escaped with a safe weighing 700 lbs (317 kg). Although the gang had to rip the safe from the wall and drag it out of the building, the theft was not discovered until the morning shift arrived.

EDIBLE WEAPON

In December 2004, a man from Oklahoma was charged with assault after trying to stab another man with a pork chop!

GHOSTLY DRIVER

A Tennessee man was ticketed for five driving violations ten days after he died.

SNAKE STOWAWAY

Like most people returning from vacation, following a 2006 trip to the Philippines, Helga Gurnsteidl from Nuremberg, Germany, put her dirty clothes in the washing machine. When she took her clean clothes out of the washing machine, however, she found a snake in them. The green ring snake—a rare Filipino native—had survived the flight to Germany as well as the spin cycle in the washer.

BOY RACER

An 11-year-old boy from Independence, Missouri, took his parents' 1995 Chevrolet and drove 200 mi (322 km), reaching speeds of 85 mph (137 km/h) before running out of gas and accidentally locking the keys in the car.

DRILL STYLIST

A man in Edmonton, Alberta, Canada, partially scalped his girlfriend by attempting to "style" her hair with a power drill—a technique he said he had learned about on TV.

HEALTH HAZARD

In Greater Manchester, England, in 2006, an office floor collapsed under the weight of a boardroom table during a meeting of 21 health and safety officers.

SHARP SURPRISE ▽

Sarita Bista from western Nepal has defied the laws of nature by pulling small triangular-shaped pieces of glass from her head every day for the past three years. The unusual 12-year-old sometimes loses conciousness when the bizarre process begins, but no serious harm seems to befall her. Her baffled doctors are seeking help from scientists to try to solve the mystery.

OLD NOODLES

Noodles unearthed on an archeological site in Lajia, China, in 2005 are reckoned to be about 4,000 years old. Unlike modern noodles, which are made from wheat flour, these were made using grains from millet grass and are thought to have been buried during a catastrophic flood.

FINGER CLUE

After breaking into a leisure center in Hamburg, Germany, Michael Baumgartner fled when police arrived—but a ring on his index finger caught on a metal fence and tore his finger off. The severed finger was found by police at the scene and matched to his prints on their database.

HOUSE DUMPED

Littering reached a whole new level along a highway in Tampa, Florida, when someone discarded the complete second floor of a three-bedroom, two-bath house beside U.S. Highway 301.

TANK RIDE

In 2006, a man drove a 12-ton tank through the historic town center of Hradec Kralove in the Czech Republic—just to buy his kids ice cream. Miroslav Tucek said he had to use the armored personnel carrier, which he bought from the Czech Army, because his car had broken down. He told police it was too far to walk from his home and he had promised his children an ice cream.

△ SKIN PORTRAIT

This portrait of Sara Fernandez is a painting with a difference, for it has been painted on the surgically removed skin of her mother. Angie Fernandez from Tucson, Arizona, had a tummy tuck in March 2006, and decided to put her skin to this unusual use. The skin, which measures 7 x 9 in (18 x 23 cm), was professionally cured before Angie's brother, Reuben Daniell, painted the portrait. It should last forever.

BLACK AND WHITE TWINS

At odds of around a million to one, these two beautiful babies are actually twins. Conceived naturally, Alicia and Jasmin Singerl from Queensland, Australia, have a mixed-race mother and a white father. In most cases, the eggs from a mixed-race woman will be a mix of genes for both black and white skin but, occasionally, the eggs carry genes for predominantly one skin color. This is what happened with the twin's mother—twice over and at the same time!

Dust Artist

Scott Wade doesn't use a conventional canvas for his works of art. Instead, he makes fantastic re-creations of old masters on the dusty rear windshield of his Mini Cooper car.

By using his fingers, paintbrushes, and even popsicle sticks, he has copied in dust such works as Leonardo da Vinci's *Mona Lisa*, Van Gogh's *Starry Night*, and C.M. Coolidge's *A Friend in Need*, which features dogs playing poker.

Scott lives on a 1½-mi (2.4-km) dirt road near San Marcos, Texas. The road is a blend of limestone dust, gravel, and clay, and driving over it produces a fine white dust behind the vehicle. When sufficient dust has collected on the

rear windshield, he uses a rubber "paint shaper" tool to mark out the drawing and then adds the shading with brushes. He achieves the contrast in light and dark gray by varying the amount of dust.

Each picture takes around an hour and he often draws them in three sessions. If he needs more dust, he simply goes for a short drive between sessions. Extra dust and morning dew ensure that the pictures constantly change. However, Scott knows that his dirty car art is only temporary. A heavy shower of rain and it just washes clean away.

Scott re-creates famous portraits and other works of art on his car's rear windshield in Texas.

THE WEIGH INN
In March 2006, the Ostfriesland Hotel in Germany began charging visitors by how much they weigh.

GRAVEDIGGER BURIED
A 62-year-old gravedigger from Nieuwleusen, the Netherlands, had a lucky escape in 2006 after accidentally burying himself. A trailer containing the earth he had removed tipped over and fell back into the grave, knocking him over and covering him completely. Fortunately, a colleague managed to scrape away the soil from the gravedigger's face so that he could breathe until rescued.

JUMBO JAM

A 40-ft (12-m) long water-spewing mechanical elephant weighing 42 tons, as much as seven African elephants, brought the center of London, England, to a standstill in May 2006. The princely pachyderm was part of a four-day street theater performance by a French arts company. The elephant, made largely of wood, consisted of hundreds of moving parts, and was operated by more than ten puppeteers using hydraulics and motors.

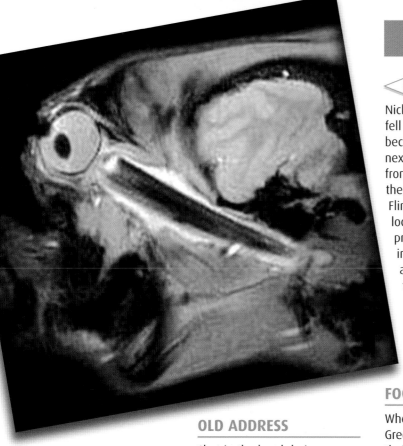

◁ IN LIKE FLINT ▷

Nicky Killeen's Weimaraner, Flint, fell on a 3-in (8-cm) stick that became lodged behind his eye next to his brain in 2006. Nicky, from Essex, England, didn't see the incident but noticed that Flint's eye was swollen. A local veterinarian initially prescribed the dog anti-inflammatory medication and antibiotics. When the treatment had no effect Flint had a scan, which revealed the large splinter. It had just missed Flint's arteries, eyeball, nerves, and brain. The splinter was removed, and Flint suffered no ill effects from his ordeal.

TOO REALISTIC

Responding to a call from a park ranger reporting a hostage situation, Colorado police arrested a number of suspects, only to discover that they were actors making a crime movie. Larimer County deputies handcuffed crew members and pointed a rifle at actor Chris Borden.

PETITE PUB

Measuring just 8 x 8 ft (2.4 x 2.4 m), the recently opened Signal Box Inn at Cleethorpes, Lincolnshire, England, is not a pub for large parties. A former railway signal box, it has four stools and standing room for another two customers.

OLD ADDRESS

Shot in the head during a robbery, Larry Taylor of Georgia then walked 2 mi (3.2 km) so he could die at his mother's house—only to find that she had moved. Larry ultimately survived the ordeal.

CAR CHASE

The driver of a stolen BMW led police on a 370-mi (595-km) car chase across southwestern Australia, driving up to 110 mph (177 km/h). He stopped only when he ran out of gas.

FOOTBALL FRENZY

When Chicago Bears beat Green Bay Packers 26–0 in their September 2006 season opener, it cost Bears' fan Randy Gonigam $300,000 in free furniture. Gonigam, owner of a Plano, Illinois, store, had offered customers free furniture up to $10,000 a head if the Bears achieved a shutout against the Packers. With 206 customers taking up the offer, it was a good job he had taken out $300,000 insurance to cover himself.

VODKA PIPELINE

In 2004, smugglers were caught bringing vodka into Lithuania from neighboring Belarus through a pipeline that was 2 mi (3.2 km) long.

CAN MOUNTAIN

In 2005, a man in Ogden, Utah, had his house cleaned after amassing 70,000 empty beer cans collected over eight years of living alone.

MIRACULOUS RECOVERY ▷

A dog in California was run over, shot, and frozen—but still lived! Dosha, a ten-month-old of mixed breeding, first ran into trouble when she was hit by a car near her owner's Clearwater home. To put her out of her misery, a police officer shot her in the head and, presumed dead, she was put in a freezer at an animal control center. Then, two hours later, a veterinarian opened the door to the freezer and was amazed to see Dosha standing upright in a plastic orange bag, the equivalent of a human body bag.

"MINOR" OFFENCE

In May 2006, police in Vancouver, British Columbia, Canada, arrested a 14-year-old boy and two 13-year-olds for robbing seven banks!

GRANNY'S JACKPOT

Just as she was about to run out of coins, grandmother Josephine Crawford won more than $10 million on a five-cent slot machine at Harrah's Atlantic City casino in New Jersey in 2006. Mrs Crawford, a widow, immediately received four marriage proposals while celebrating her good fortune.

HOUNDED OUT

An elderly Polish man was chained up by his wife in a dog kennel for three weeks in 2006 because she was angry with him repeatedly arriving home drunk on vodka. The 75-year-old man had to survive in freezing temperatures wrapped in an old blanket and existing on dog food and water. He was freed only after his drinking friends, concerned by his absence, informed the police.

PILLOW TALK

An Indian man was ordered to leave his wife in 2006 after he said "talaq"—the Arabic equivalent of "I divorce you"— three times in his sleep.

2,000 YEARS △ TOO LATE

A German art student joined the Chinese terracotta army in the city of Xi'an almost 2,200 years too late! Pablo Wendel donned a costume that matched uniforms worn by the soldiers buried in the tomb of Emperor Qin Shihuangdi, who ruled between 221 and 210BC. He slipped past security at the museum and into the pit where 2,000 warriors are on display. Security staff took a few minutes to find him standing still among his fellow warriors.

HOT PANTS

Fleeing after robbing a Bank of America branch in Tampa, Florida, in 2006, a man stuffed the bag of cash down his pants. The chemical dye included in the bag in order to permanently mark thieves then exploded, creating a temperature of around 425°F (218°C)!

GATOR GOD

This alligator belonging to Michael Wilks from Salem, Wisconsin, clearly has the letters "G O D" marked on its side. The letters became visible once the gator reached three years of age.

PORSCHE PRANK

Greg Good, the Carolina Panthers fan who dresses up as Catman at the football team's home games, was excited at the prospect of winning a Porsche in a TV station's competition, but it turned out that the prize was a toy Porsche. When station bosses realized that the on-air practical joke had backfired on them badly, they presented Good with a pickup truck as consolation prize.

DOGGY NUPTIALS

A female Great Dane and male Pug dog had their union blessed by Reverend Charlotte Richards in the petal-strewn Little White Wedding Chapel in Selfridge's department store in London, England, in April 2005. The bride wore a white lace veil and white paw bands.

SURPRISE CATCH

In August 2005, Alan Chaplaski, a fisherman from Stonington, Connecticut, was trawling for shrimp when he snagged a U.S. Navy nuclear submarine 362 ft (110 m) long!

SEEING DOUBLE ▽

Retired lifeguard Michael Morris from Cornwall, England, got more than he bargained for when making an omelette for his lunch one day in April 2006. Cracking a particularly large egg into a bowl (hoping he'd maybe bought a double-yolker), Morris was amazed when a smaller egg fell out. His egg-within-an-egg has been described as extremely rare by experts.

SLIM CHANCE

A prisoner dieted his way to freedom in Australia by squeezing through a narrow gap after losing more than 30 lbs (13.6 kg). He had weighed 154 lbs (70 kg) when jailed in 2003 but because he had slimmed down to 124 lbs (56 kg) in the intervening two years, he was able to escape through a space he had chiseled between the wall and the bars on his cell window.

HIGH DINING △

A group of 22 Belgian chefs took part in an extreme dining experience in Brussels in April 2006. Strapped into racing-car seats, they enjoyed a three-course meal while suspended from a crane 165 ft (50 m) high above the streets of Belgium's capital city.

PINK HANDCUFFS

In 2005, police officers in Maricopa County, Arizona, began using fluorescent pink handcuffs when making arrests!

FAKED DEATH

A woman from Des Moines, Iowa, allegedly faked her own death to avoid paying parking fines. She apparently wrote her own obituary, made to look like a page from the website of the *Des Moines Register*, and forged a letter informing a judge that she had died in a car crash. But she was caught out after she was given yet another parking ticket just a month after her "death."

PIZZA HERO

While dressed in cape and tights as superhero "Luke Pie-Rocker" for his pizza delivery job, Cameron Evans of Minneapolis, Minnesota, foiled a purse snatching in June 2006.

DOG DISTRACTION

Police in Stockton-on-Tees, England, investigated a bizarre burglary in 2006 in which one of the thieves pretended to be a dog. Two men barged into a house owned by a brother and sister in their nineties, and while one of the thieves dropped to his knees and started to crawl around on all fours and bark like a dog, his accomplice grabbed the woman's purse.

PYTHON PACKAGE

Staff at a post office in Mechernich, Germany, were horrified to see a 5-ft (1.5-m) albino python escape from a parcel. The package, labeled "Attention—Glass," had been accepted by the staff and put in the back of the office. But then it started to move and the large snake slithered out of the wrapping.

FAKE FUR

In 2004, a high-tech X-ray machine at Chicago's Field Museum revealed that a mummified cat on display was actually a 2,500-year-old fraud made of cotton and twigs.

PORK TALK

Karim Tiro of Xavier University in Cincinnati, Ohio, teaches a college-level class on the history of pigs in America.

SERIAL OFFENDER

By 2003, Alison Graham of Halifax, Nova Scotia, Canada, had collected 229 parking fines totaling $10,000 in just a couple of years.

FATHER'S FOLLY

Troy Stewart's plan to cure his 10-year-old daughter's fear of heights backfired when he broke his leg as the pair jumped into water from a 15-ft (4.5-m) bridge in Lantana, Florida, in September 2006. While Stewart writhed in pain, the uninjured Meagan cycled home to fetch help.

WINNING BET

When England national soccer team goalkeeper Chris Kirkland made his international soccer debut against Greece in August 2006, he earned his father Eddie $20,000. Eddie had bet $200 at 100–1 in 1997 that his son, then aged 15, would one day play for England's national team.

FOOD HAUL

An escaped prisoner was caught trying to get back into Roane County Jail, Tennessee, in 2005 with four McDonald's hamburgers. The man, who had escaped for only a short time, was found carrying a package containing liquor, prescription pills, clothes, and the burgers.

POISONED PIGEONS

The 2006 city festival at Texarkana, Texas, was marred when more than 25 sick or dead pigeons nose-dived onto downtown sidewalks. They had apparently eaten poisoned corn from the roof of a nearby bank.

COZY COFFIN

Kay Groom keeps a coffin in the spare bedroom of her home in Swaffham, Norfolk, England, and likes to take the mystery out of death by lying in it. Kay who also has a collection of more than 300 ornamental skulls and admits to being fascinated by death, was measured for the $400 satin-lined pine box a few years ago. "It's the coffin I'm going to buried in," she says. "It's very comfy, although I don't like it with the lid down because I'm a bit claustrophobic. People think I'm mad, macabre, and some think I'm a witch. But I'm not."

Index

ACKNOWLEDGMENTS

COVER (t/l) The University of Manchester, (b/r) Courtesy of Juan Cabana; 4 Davison Design and Development www.inventionland.com; 6–7 (dp, t) Courtesy of Juan Cabana; 8 PA Photos; 9 (l) Davison Design and Development www.inventionland.com; 10 (b) Stewart Cook/Rex Features, (t) The University of Manchester; 11 (t) Nils Jorgensen/Rex Features, (b) Rex Features; 12–13 (t) 2daymedia; 12 (b) William Kennedy/Ripley Entertainment Inc.; 13 (b) Reuters/Stringer India; 14 (t/l) Great Plains Regional Medical Center, (b) PA Photos; 15 (c) PA Photos, (b) Reuters/Anthony Bolante; 16 (b) Reuters/Rupak De Chowdhuri; 17 (t) Matt Cardy/Getty Images, (b) Stan Honda/AFP/Getty Images; 18 (t) The Davey Tree Expert Company, (b) Reuters/Stringer Thailand; 19 Brandy Conley/Ripley Entertainment Inc.; 21 (t) Camera Press/Wu Fang/ChinaFotoPress, (b) Charles Hasley/Ripley Entertainment Inc.; 22 (t/r) ChinaFotoPress/Zhao Haijiang/UPPA/Photoshot, (b) Rex Features; 23 (t/l) 2daymedia, (t/r) Camera Press/Wattie Cheung, (c/l) Mark Clifford/Barcroft Media, (c/r) Camera Press/Yang Wanjiang/Phototex, (b/l) Jamie Jones/Rex Fetures, (b/r) Gong Hui/UPPA/Photoshot; 24 Newscom; 25 (t) Sara Fernandez/Ripley Entertainment Inc., (b) Jamie Hanso/Newspix/Rex Features; 26 (t/r, t/c/l) Scott Wade, (t/c/r) Jules Alexander, (b/c, b) Scott Wade; 27 (t/r) Scott Wade, (t/c/l) Jules Alexander, (c) Scott Wade, (b) John McDavitt; 28 Reuters/Stephen Hird; 29 (t) Peter Lawson/Rex Features; 30 (t) Reuters/China Daily China Daily Information Corp—CDIC, (b) Michael Wilks/Ripley Entertainment Inc.; 31 Chris Jackson/Getty Images; 32 (t) Reuters/Francois Lenoir, (b) 2daymedia; 33 PA Photos

All other photos are from Corel, PhotoDisc, Digital Vision and Ripley's Entertainment Inc.